SUNSHINE OF MY VERSES

HARENDER SAINI

This book is dedicated to my father Late Mr. Jagir Singh who had always wanted me to do something extraordinary. He educated me in a boarding school St. Mary's Convent, Nainital, where I developed excellent writing skills that have enabled me to write this book. I miss him a lot.

Contents

Contents

Acknowledgements

I am highly thankful to my parents - my father Late Mr. Jagir Singh and my mother Mrs. Kulwant Kaur for providing me with an excellent education to write this book. I'm also thankful to my son Ranbir and my friends who motivated me to write.

1. A Bouquet of Roses

A bouquet of roses I will always treasure
Sent with good wishes beyond measure
Made me happy to have a friend
Who sent it from a land the other end
Shades of pink a sweet aroma
Filled my heart with happiness
The kind gesture I will always treasure
I'm fortunate to have her beyond measure.

2. A Friend

A friend is one who is yours in times of need
Stands by your side in your hard days.
And holds your hand in grief
She gives you confidence and motivates you
To go ahead in your life
Lucky are those who have true friends
In this world such are hard to find
There are those who are with you if you are powerful
Or your pockets are full to enjoy and make merry
And then forget you
This is the truth of present times
A true friend is hard to find.

3. The Mulberry Tree

In the garden we had a mulberry tree

It was big and had green leaves

We gathered there every evening to play

When a rope was tied to its branches

To and fro we swayed.

From March to May and October to November

The tree was laden with purple and crimson berries

We would relish them with delight and jump merrily

In the evening the tree was our favourite place

We would lean against the trunk and tell our tales

One day to our dismay it was uprooted

A cobra had upwards shooted

It became his home and a danger for us

We accepted it without a fuss

Deep in our hearts we missed the days

When we relished the mulberries and swayed

On the rope tied to the branches of the majestic tree

We will always cherish the beautiful memories .

4. A Pigeon on my Window Sill

On a hot summer noon
I drew the curtains aside
To see the green leaves
Of the trees outside.

I saw a pigeon looking at me
Moving about the window sill
His beak hit the window pane
As if to say I'm here again.

I opened the balcony door
And put a bowl of water
He quenched his thirst with delight
When cooler he took a short flight.

The green purple sheen glistened in the sun
He flew for a short while and returned for more fun
He ran on the window sill pecking at the glass
Flapping his wings to thank me and happily began to run.

5. Autumn

Autumn is my favourite season
For this there are many reasons.
After the hot summer it is welcomed
With picnics trekking before the winter months .

The clear blue sky with seldom a white cloud
Birds busy making nests for the winter around.
Gold rust leaves are strewn along the path
Busy ants carry food so they don't have to fast.

The breeze blows with more force
Making people close all doors.
The chill in the air increases day by day
So winter is not far away.

6. Stormy Day

Trees are swaying from end to end
as if they would break only to be
held firmly by the strong roots
embedded in the ground.

Sounds of doors banging can be heard
window panes rattle , the glass about to break
roof tops seem to be blown off
leaves, hay and swirls of dust fill the air.

Ladies hold their skirts and hats
rushing indoors to be safe
from the dreadful storm that has
caused such havoc and restlessness.

The fury of nature is uncertain
controlled by a supreme power
it comes and goes causing great devastation
to life on earth.

7. Home

Sound sleep with pleasant dreams engulf me

I wake up to the chirp of birds,

Mother serves me delicious food every morsel of which
I relish

The fresh gushing water of the stream

nearby tempts me to wade in it,

I see tiny fish in the crystal clear water swimming
perhaps to reach the ocean.

I walk upward along the stream

huge boulders block my path,

I can hear the waterfall

I shout and to my amazement I hear the echo of my

voice.

A huge black furry creature walks in the thicket

to perhaps drink the sweet nectar of the waterfall,

It turns and starts towards me, I charge downstream

breathless only to find myself in front of my home.

I bolt the door and relax in the safe enclosure

where no harm can enter,

Mother's caring voice makes me embrace her

I nestle in her arms sure of safety and love.

8. Innocence

I saw an innocent baby
Who made me think for a while
She had a smile
So tender and mild.

I had never seen a face so bright
That I was inspired to write
Her sparkling eyes held my gaze
I kept on looking at her face.

Her innocence made my heart sing
It seemed no gem could match the infant
So adorable and sweet was she
Her face remains in my memory.

Her name was Bess
I thought she was a princess
God bless her who charmed me so much
I wish her a long life and a lot of fun.

9. Inspiration

Living in solitude for almost a year
I was sad and depressed
When one evening I heard a chirpy voice
A voice full of life and cheer
It was of a girl not more than seven or eight
Shrill and chirpy it elated my spirits
I longed to see her but could not
I heard her talk every evening
It brought a song in my heart and a smile on my face
I hope to meet the cheerful one some day
Who made me glad in every way
after almost a year of solitude and sadness.

10. Life

A white sheet still over
the surroundings.
As I hover closer
trees are faintly visible.
only the vehicle horns can be
heard in the distance.
A cold breeze lifts it
the sun rays try to
heal the earth,
birds begin to chirp.
People come out relieved
thankful that the cold
sheet has vanished into thin air
making way for warmth.

11. Morning

The first rays of the sun
kiss the dew on the soft grass
which glistens like a precious gem.
Sweet fragrance of the blooms
the buzzing of bees fill the air,
Butterflies of yellow and orange hues and
birds fly in the clear blue sky
As if to conquer the mountains close by.

12. Mother

I would not have been here without you mother
You cannot replace any sister or brother
You carried me for nine months with you
Always worried if I was fine in you.

You were with me when I crawled around
Fed me with cereals milk and juice
Stayed awake till I slept sound
Changed my wet nappies all night through.

My first word and step brought delight to your face
Holding my hand you walked with grace
My smile and mischief made you glad
My illness made you worried and sad.

You are everything for me mother
I am here today because of you and no other
I pray to God to keep you well and strong
And make you my mother all along.

13. Night

Darkness everywhere

Glow worms shine

Owls hoot, jackals howl

Crickets sing.

Hyenas yawn and laugh

their time to have a feast.

Trees whisper in the gentle breeze

Stars twinkle the moon is at ease.

Water of the stream sparkles

Sounds of ripples add beauty to the night

Bats screech, the fox cries

A roar is heard

Everything is disturbed

The quiet of the night goes by.

14. Spring

Come spring and life begins

Tender leaves sprout

Birds begin to sing.

Blossom fragrance fills the air

Buds unfurl into different hues

Flitting butterflies, buzzing of bees

clear skies fresh green trees

add to the beauty of spring.

Reptiles wake up from their sleep

Children play hide and seek.

Laughter and joy fill the air

Spring thrills there's no despair.

15. Summer

Come April and summer starts

The dreadful days of sweat and grime

Leaving the freshness of spring far behind.

The hot sun up in the sky

Makes lips and mouth turn dry.

Not a sound of birds is heard

They are nestled in trees after quenching their thirst.

Squirrels are seen running about nibbling flowers

Not a leaf is swaying everything is still

The humming of bees has gone with spring

Melons, litchies and mangoes are in plenty

Squashes and pickles fill the jars that were empty.

Variety of fruits add cheer to the summer

A storm or two are followed by showers

which cool the earth from the sweltering heat

Cotton and linen are the cool attire

Floral designs add colour to the hot days of fire

Days are too long the sun too bright

In summer the starlit sky is a beautiful sight

Glow worms flying and the crickets singing with delight.

16. Sunset

I was on the cliff overlooking the sea

A gentle breeze gushed past me,

When I looked ahead I saw

A majestic sight as never before,

A huge red ball sinking into the waves

Pushing them aside as if for space.

The sky changed to shades of orange, yellow and red

Calling the birds to return to their nests.

I looked up to see parrots sparrows by the dozen

Flying across the sky turned golden.

The red ball had almost sunk into the sea

Chirps stopped and silence spread around the trees.

I heard the water gushing against the shore,

The cricket began to sing along

The hoot of an owl and purr of a cat

Made me finally put on my hat

I traced my steps homeward

With memories of the golden world.

17. Me

A slender girl with a pleasing smile

Thick lustrous jet black hair braided

neatly, clear pearl-like complexion

rosy cheeks, doe-like eyes a nose well shaped.

A true beauty many would admire

and look at endlessly.

A woman out to tread into the world

with a cautious step to begin a new life.

Perfect in her profession, loved by all

for her gentle ways.

A soft-hearted mother sacrificing her life

to bring up her bundle of joy.

A grey-haired middle-aged beauty

still active despite the joints giving way.

Never ready to accept her declining stage

determined to be the best in her endeavours.

Perfection is her motto and perfect she will be

till she can no longer have control over herself.

18. The Butterfly

I woke up from a deep sleep

My wings are new to fly

I was an ugly Caterpillar

All said passing by

Now I'm a beautiful butterfly

My wings are orange and black

I drink the sweet nectar

Of flowers big and small

From flower to flower I fly

Escaping the nets the children try

To imprison me forever

I fly up as if to heaven

Safe and sound

Thankful to my wings

That carry me up and down

And I'm free forever.

19. The Cobra

A spectacled head swaying

The long sleek black tapering body

A majestic sight to behold

The cobra moves about the simbal tree

Birds shrieking crows cawing

Aloft the straight branches

Heralding the presence of the black king

It moves in a wriggling motion

Tries to feel the reverberating cries

Comes back to the foot of the simbal

And sits still in a coiled ring

With the hood raised above

Turning left and right to view the scene

As if sensing danger

The forked tongue flicking in and out

Of the wide mouth baring venomous fangs

Which when struck bring an end to life

It retreats into the crevice in the wall

Probably to come out again for a stroll

Amidst the grass around the old simbal.

20. The Gentle Breeze

A gentle breeze blew

Bringing relief to all

The sultry weather went for a while

A smile spread on passersby

Enjoying the short lived freshness

That one experiences during the rains

*Birds flitted on the boughs which
danced once again*

Everywhere was a song

Of laughter and joy

It was soon over

when out came the sun

Spreading its warm air

stopping all the fun.

21. The Lofty Pines

I remember the tall pines

When I went to boarding school

Tall and sturdy with needle like leaves

That fell on the ground like a golden sheet

Hay we called it while we played

Beautiful cones fell and wood roses too

We collected them in our pinafore

Preserved them like treasure

Out numbering each other was a pleasure

A unique fragrance lingered in the air

In and out we breathed the fresh air

When the branches made a whispering sound

And swayed about left and right

We knew a storm was around

The lofty pines were sturdy and strong

Withstood all severe storms

Slanting branches gave them a conical shape

Adding to their beauty never to fade.

22. The Meadow

I went to the meadow at dawn

The green grass looked like a well spread carpet

Leaves of the birches and oaks were scattered everywhere.

As the first rays of the sun appeared in the sky

*the silence was broken by the cawing of the ravens and the
chirping of birds*

nature was awake.

The deep blue sky was speckled with white clouds

Butter cups and daisies in yellow and white hues

the pink blossoms of peaches and cherries

made nature bloom to the full.

A gentle breeze blew as the sun turned from orange to yellow

The dewdrops on the butter cups and daisies sparkled like diamonds.

Colourful butterflies flew around the dancing sunrays

made the dewdrops glitter on the meadow.

I watched the serene environment taking deep breaths of the fresh air

listening to the sounds of nature as if I was in paradise

I thanked Almighty for his wonderful creation

Wishing life was always like the meadow.

23. The Ocean

The gentle blue ocean waters

seem to meet the horizon

I sit down to gaze at the

white dots coming towards the shore.

The sails of fishing boats are visible

as they come closer.

Smiles on the faces of fishermen are
certain of a great catch in the nets.

Looking upto heaven as if thanking
God for his grace

anchor their boats on the shore against
the setting orange glow of the evening.

24. The Rain

Pitter patter sounds are heard
As rain falls from the sky
A relief for the scorching earth
and birds who happily fly.

Dark clouds float above
The breeze is pleasant and cool
Prickly heat, sweat and grime
Vanish with the drops sublime.

Trees and plants are washed clean
appear in various shades of green
With songs in the heart
the farmers plough the fields.

Everything is full of life
with a spell of rain
Hands are folded in a prayer
Nothing goes in vain.

25. The Rainbow

The rain stopped
Sunrays peeped
Out came a rainbow
As beautiful as can be

The colourful band spread across the sky
Impossible to touch as it was so high
Seven beautiful colours were in the band
This was nature's hand.

All young and old
Came out to see
Dancing and singing
As merry as can be.

And as the story goes
At the end of it lies a pot of gold
How true it is we don't know
It is the story of the rainbow.

26. The Wild

Acacia trees grow here and there amidst the tall dense savanna
grasslands

Thorny bushes accompanied by cacti

All forming a camouflage for animals to protect themselves from
predators

How wonderful is God's creation.

The wild leaves me spellbound,

Eyes are filled with amazement at the agile leap of the cheetah

in an attempt of preying the fawn

Like a flash of lightning the timid life is gone and the cheetah
has his
fill.

A roar in the distance makes the animals run for shelter else
they fall prey to predators.

Laugh of hyenas and trumpets of tuskers add to the cacophony of
the wild

The red blaze of the setting sun makes the sky appear as if it's on
fire

It's an alarm for the animals to return to their dwellings and the
nocturnal creatures to come out.

The beauty of the wild yearns my heart to remain there forever

amidst the blissful creation of God.

27. The Woodpecker

A gulmohar stood tall in my garden

Something hit the tree trunk

I looked up and saw a woodpecker

Whose work had begun.

She pecked at the wood

with a strong pointed beek

She pecked again and again

down fell a piece of wood

A home she had made to sleep sound

She went inside and peeped out

Satisfied to say it was well made.

Beautiful she was with a crown on her head

Took a short flight

Came back in delight

Welcomed her friends to join her

Soon wings flapped and danced around

Bidding adieu they all went

after a good feast

Hoping to come again for another treat

In the woodpecker's home on the tree.

28. The Pine Forest

I remember the Pine forest we visited in our school days
during the week long summer holidays
In pairs we walked downhill ,then on the mettled road
Soon we arrived the turn to climb up to the pine forest.

Pines of all sizes loaded with cones were there in plenty
The hillside looked beautiful with golden pine needles strewn
around
There were cones lying about and wood roses too
The sun shone overhead in the sky that was blue.

Fragrance of the pines filled the air
Butter cups and daisies grew in plenty
The buzzing of bees and flitting of butterflies
Added a new life to the hillside .

We sat down to eat by the stream
The cool clear water glistened in the bright sun
Blind man's buff and passing the parcel we played
It was soon time to wind up and call it a day.

Back in our rows we went

Trudging downhill and then climbing up
Reached our school exhausted and sleepy
The memories of the pine forest still fresh and worth keeping.

29. Time

Everything changes with the passage of time
Nothing remains forever sublime
An infant becomes old
The beautiful rose withers
Do good and harm none
From good deeds do not dither
Time passes age catches
Everything comes to an end
Make peace have no hatred
Remain a true friend
Tis true time doesn't come back
It moves on and on
With it nothing returns
Before you realize all is gone.

30. Unrest

The youth are under pressure
Cannot tolerate anyone above their measure
Helter skelter up and down
Each is smart and duty bound
Not satisfied with their earnings
Switch jobs very early
Difficult to adjust
They are their own judge
Mood swings are common
They laugh and shout often
Quick succession is what they seek
Not knowing it's too bleak
Electronic gadgets are a part of life
Without them they cannot survive
Top brands are a trend
In fashion at the end
Today's youth are full of zest
Under pressure and unrest.

31. Villager

A simple dwelling, in a calm serene environment

lives a man in a three room house with a courtyard
surrounded by a boundary wall.

The urban lot call him a villager
due to his simplicity.

An early riser takes rounds of his fields

which probably the urban people would never
dream of having.

The fresh air, greenery all around,

birds chirping in the trees squirrels running about,

Cows and buffaloes in plenty are part of his life.

Fresh milk, good flour, fresh vegetables he eats

he is a strong man with a turban tied on his head

ready to help all he can, always welcomes people to his house.

The villager is looked down upon considered a loud rustic

but he is more energetic and generous than the city dweller.

32. War

Troops marching tanks moving
Sirens blaring people screaming
Missiles striking buildings falling
Smoke filled skies
Moanings and cries
Blood and bodies everywhere
Animals and humans together
Lying all scattered
A deathly silence fills the air
Horrors of war dreadful to bear.